Royal Icing

75g (3oz) Dried albumen
500ml (1 pint) Cold water
3kg (7lb) Icing sugar
25g (1oz) Glycerine (optional)

Dissolve the dried albumen into the cold water, leave for two hours.

Place into a grease free bowl on your food mixer fitted with a beater, (This is very important to insure best results).

Gradually add the icing sugar on slow speed, beating till a firm peak is obtained.

Slowly add the glycerine (optional) till fully mixed into the royal icing.

Adding glycerine gives a better cutting quality to your cakes, you do not add this in the making of Pastillage.

Pastillage

500g, Royal Icing Made with no glycerine added
2 teaspoons (10 ml) Gum tragacanth
500g, icing sugar *(you may need a little more or a little less to suit your needs).*

Place the royal icing into a grease free bowl; add the gum tragacanth and stir in slowly, then add the icing sugar mixing with your hands until it forms soft dough.

Place this in a polythene bag and store in a plastic container with a lid for 24 hours. This can last up to three weeks if left in a refrigerator.

Filling Cream

500g Good quality margarine
500g Block fondant *(available from good sugarcraft shops).*

Place the margarine into a mixer fitted with a beater. Cut the block fondant into small squares and add to the margarine a little at a time on slow speed till blended together.

Increase the speed on the mixer to high speed and beat for 15 minutes till the mixture has gone lighter in colour and fluffier.

Icing sugar can replace block fondant if you wish, using the same quantity. If you require a more whiter filling there is white cake margarine on the market, just ask your local sugarcraft shop. Using a white margarine gives you true colours when colouring for swirls on cupcakes.

Contents

You will need:
20cm (8") oval sponge cake
10cm (4") square sponge cake
30cm (12") Cake drum square
Cake smoother
Edible glue
1kg, White sugarpaste
250g, Black sugarpaste
Small amounts of Yellow/ brown/pale green sugarpaste
300g, Pale peach coloured sugarpaste
Silver spangle or snowflake cake dust
Paint brush
Rejuvenating spirit
Edible spray glaze
Royal icing in black and white

Preparation

Carve the shape of the bath with a knife, a little at a time from the top and working your way down, once completed mask with filling cream place in refrigerator for about an hour to set.

1 Cut out square shapes in black and white sugarpaste and place onto the cake drum securing with edible glue, once completed spray with edible spray glaze
2 Take about 100g of the white sugarpaste and roll into a sausage shape, place this around top edge of the cake and mask with filling cream.
3 Roll out white sugarpaste and place over the cake, carefully smooth with palms of your hands and using a cake smoother.
4 To make the baby, cut to size and wet a plastic dowel with edible glue, insert into the cake. Roll a ball of peach coloured sugarpaste and place onto the dowel slightly shape to form a body and a neck, leave for about two hours to set.
   For the arms roll a sausage shape slightly thinner at one end and press to form the hands, cut to make the fingers with a craft knife, securing onto the body with edible glue. When making the head you will need to roll out a ball of sugarpaste, slightly indent the centre with your finger, mark the eyes by pressing with the end of a paint brush or a small ball tool, brush the cheeks with suitable edible dusting powder, secure the head onto the dowel, shape the mouth with a craft knife, finish the eyes with small sugarpaste balls.

Do the same for the ears indenting with the end of a paint brush, finish off by painting the eyebrows and hair with watered down food colouring.
5 Roll various sizes of ball shapes with sugarpaste to make the bubbles, placing around the baby and onto the floor securing with edible glue.
   Make shimmer paint by adding rejuvenating spirit with pearl white shimmer dust, or a like for like. Paint onto the bubbles giving a shimmery effect
6 Making the cabinet rabbit and accessories
   Cabinet: cut and shape a sponge cake, mask with filling cream and place in to fridge for one hour to set. Cover with sugarpaste, roll and cut out sugarpaste shapes to form the doors, rolling small balls for the handles.
   Rabbit: roll a ball and form into a pear shape for the body, place next to the bath; roll a ball for the head and a smaller ball and place this on top.
   Place a small piece of hard spaghetti through the body and secure the head to the body. Roll a sausage shape for the arms and legs and to make the feet roll two small pieces of sugarpaste and press with your finger and thumb. Shape the ears, securing both with edible glue, pipe the eyes with black royal icing; make a bow to finish off.
   Accessories: duck, roll a ball of sugarpaste to form a pear shape tweak the end to form the shape, roll a small ball for the head, secure on to the body and make the small wings add the beak and pipe on his eyes.
   To make the folded towels, roll a piece of sugarpaste and cut into small squares and fold over.

Finally it is nice to add your own touches, for example how about a favourite toy. Finish the edge of board by attaching ribbon colour of your choice.

You will need:
20cm (8") Square sponge cake
15cm (6") Square sponge cake
2 x 40cm (16") Square cake drums
2kg White sugarpaste
2.5kg Pale pink sugarpaste
Small amounts of, Red, Orange, Green, Blue, Purple, Deep pink, Sugarpaste
250g Pale blue Sugarpaste
500g Royal icing
Fmm Straight tool set no 2
500g pink coloured pastillage
Craft knife
Pallet knife
Spray gun and colours
Edible glue
Paint brush

Firstly you will have to make your pastillage turrets, you will need to make five large, one medium and four small.
Cover some rolled pastillage around a piece of tubing and leave to dry for 24 hours before removing the tube. Cut out circles that will later be placed on top of the turrets.

Preparation

Jam and cream the two square cakes, mask with filling cream put into the freezer until firm.
I have coloured the sugarpaste myself as I wanted it to match the pastillage turrets.
Roll out your sugarpaste place the frozen cake on top of this, cut around the cake, smooth and then start on to the sides, doing this gives your cake a nice sharp edge, leave until set.

1 Place the cake onto the centre of the cake drum, secure the smaller cake on top of the larger cake, using royal icing as glue.
2 Secure the turrets onto the sides of the bottom cake and also onto the top cake, place the cut out circles on top of these and place the smaller turrets on top securing with royal icing, it's better to leave to set before adding the upper part.
3 †o make the pointed roofs of the turrets, you will need six, roll a small ball of sugar paste place this into the palm of your hands and shape into a pear shape, tweak the top slightly to make it more pointed, secure onto the top of the turrets with edible glue.

4 Make a template for your windows and door. Roll out some sugarpaste and with a craft knife cut out and secure onto the cake with edible glue, pipe around the windows using a no2 tube to finish.
5 Roll out a sheet of pink sugarpaste and using the fmm straight tool set, cut out and place the pattern onto the top sides of the cake using the sharp edges as a guide, doing the same onto the turrets, you can finish off with small loops made with royal icing using a no 2 tube.
6 Making the clouds, take a piece of sugarpaste and form into a ball, slightly flatten with your hands and secure onto the cake board using different sizes of clouds to make it look more realistic, marking with your fingers to give it a more fluffy look. Start spraying with a spray gun using a mixture of blue and black.

Making the back drop

Cover a 40cm (16") cake drum with pale blue sugarpaste securing with edible glue.
To make the rainbow roll out long sausage shapes of colours, press with the palm of your hands to flatten secure onto the board curving into the rainbow shape. Pipe on the clouds making them look fluffy using a palate knife. Using carpet tacks hammer your two boards together to finish the theme.

Finally make the little flags for the tops of the turrets, roll small balls of sugarpaste into a pear shape and flatten with your finger and thumb into a flag shape, secure with edible glue.

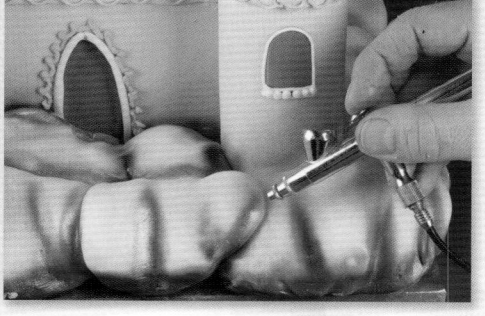

Sweet Dreams

You will need:
20cm (8") Square sponge cake
30cm (12") Square cake drum
1kg (2lb) White sugarpaste
500g (1lb) Baby blue sugarpaste
250g (8oz) Peach sugarpaste
Cake smoother
Craft knife
Paint brush
Edible glue

Firstly, roll out and cover a 12" cake drum with baby blue sugarpaste, securing with edible glue.

Preparation

Jam and cream the square cake and chill in the freezer for about one hour.
Using a 20cm (8") round card, place on to the edge of the cake and carve the curved shape, you need to do this on all four sides. Start carving the cake a little at a time you can also rub your hands across the cake to get the rounded edges and a smoother finish. Turn the cake upside down and repeat carving the cake. Mask with filling cream and chill in a refrigerator for about one hour.

1 Roll out and cover the pillow shaped cake with white sugarpaste, carefully smooth with a cake smoother and using the palms of your hands. Place on to the iced board ready for finishing.
2 Making the rope: With white sugarpaste and using the palms of your hands, start rolling quite thinly till a large sausage shape is achieved, cut this in half and place them side by side and start twisting together, till a rope is achieved. Place onto the four sides of the pillow securing with edible glue.
3 For the tassels take a small piece of sugarpaste, roll into a ball and shape this into a long pear shape, flatten this with your finger and thumb, start marking with the back of a knife to make the string effect. You will need to make four, secure onto the corners with edible glue.
4 To make the bows, roll out some white sugarpaste and cut into small strips using a craft knife, fold each end till they meet in the middle press the middle forming the bow, place onto the cake securing with edible glue.

How to make the baby

Remember a baby's head needs to be quite large and more round in shape, the facial features tend to be small and concentrate on the centre of the face.

I tend to make the body first, take a piece of sugarpaste about 125g (4oz) and roll into a ball. With the palms of your hands mould into a pear shape place this onto a flat surface and press the slimmer end, secure onto the pillow with edible glue.

To make the head, roll a ball with peach sugarpaste press the centre of the ball with your finger to make an indent. Dust the cheeks with a suitable edible dusting powder, roll a sausage shape for the arms slightly tweak the inside of one end to form a dip, this is where the hand will go, the same method for making the arms is the same for the legs, the only difference being is moulding the feet, by pressing with your finger and thumb and bending to form.

For the hands: roll a ball with sugarpaste form into a pear shape; press this with your finger and thumb, cut to form the fingers with a craft knife.

It's nice to add little features, such as a little bonnet and the buttons and piped bows I have painted the hair using watered down food colouring, all ads to the handmade nature of your cake.

Finishing touches: add piped pearls with a No 2 tube on to the pillow, do the same on the cake board, giving it a more professional look.

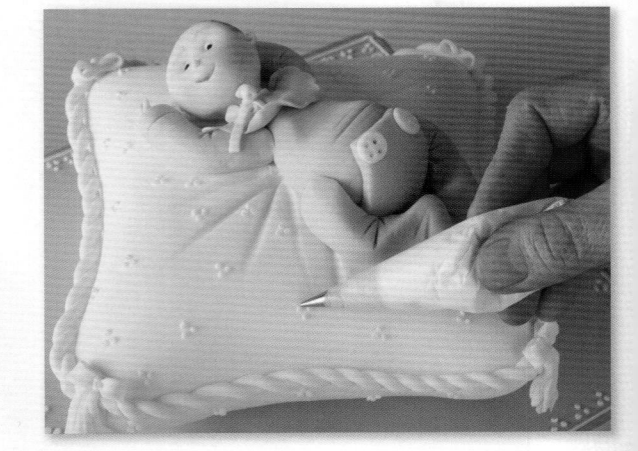

You will need:
3 x 10cm (4") fruit cakes
(30cm) 12" Cake drum
1kg (2lb) marzipan
750g (1lb 8oz) White sugarpaste
750g (1lb 8oz) brown coloured sugarpaste
250g (8oz) red sugarpaste
500g (1lb) royal icing
250g (8oz) pastillage
Spray gun and colours
No 2 Piping tube

Firstly, cover the cake drum with white icing. To make the bird footprints, take the end of a piece of wire and bend into a small L shape, while the icing is still soft emboss into the icing three times making the prints, you will need to do this later on top of the roof.

Preparation

Cut the roof shape from one of the square cakes then stacks together securing with boiled apricot jam.

Making the branches

Roll long thin sausage shapes with brown coloured pastillage, cut the ends with a craft knife, to give them a more realistic look score with the back of a knife to make the bark effect. To give them more definition place onto folded tissue paper to dry normally takes 24 hours.

1 Mask the sides of the cake with apricot jam, Roll out the marzipan the depth of each side and place onto the cake trim if necessary, repeat on all four sides.
2 Cover the cake the exactly as above, using clear alcohol to secure. Emboss the wood panels with the back of a knife, do this on all four sides.
3 Cut out a circle on the cake, using a round cutter just under the roof, while the icing is still soft, this is where the robin will sit.
4 Start to spray with a spay gun, It's better to practice first on a piece of paper to get the feel, using brown firstly and adding black for the darker areas, I also add a touch of green making it look more authentic. You can use cake dusts although this may take a little longer, it can still give the same effect.

5 Once fully dry place your cake onto the iced board, Start adding royal icing and stippling, giving a snow effect.
6 Roll out some white sugarpaste and place onto the roof of the house, rubbing the edges with your finger to give it a more curved look, making it look like freshly fallen snow.

To make the robins

Roll some brown sugarpaste into a ball mould this into a pear shape; slightly tweak the end giving it the bird shape. Roll a small ball for the head, shape a small pear shape and flatten for the wings, do the same for the red breast. Hard spaghetti is used as a support, place the robins onto the cake securing with edible glue, leave to dry for one hour and add the hat.

Finishing touches: Start adding the branches, finish off by piping white royal icing on top.

For the icicles use white royal icing, I have pressure piped with a pulling down motion.

To make the holly wreath

Roll a pastillage hollow circle shape and leave to dry.

Cut a V shape out of a piping bag, fill with green royal icing start piping small leaves and leave to dry before piping the berries, add a small bow to finish.

To make the watering can

Roll sugarpaste into a large sausage shape cut to size, add the handle and spout using hard spaghetti for support.

I have finished by securing red ribbon around the edge of the board.

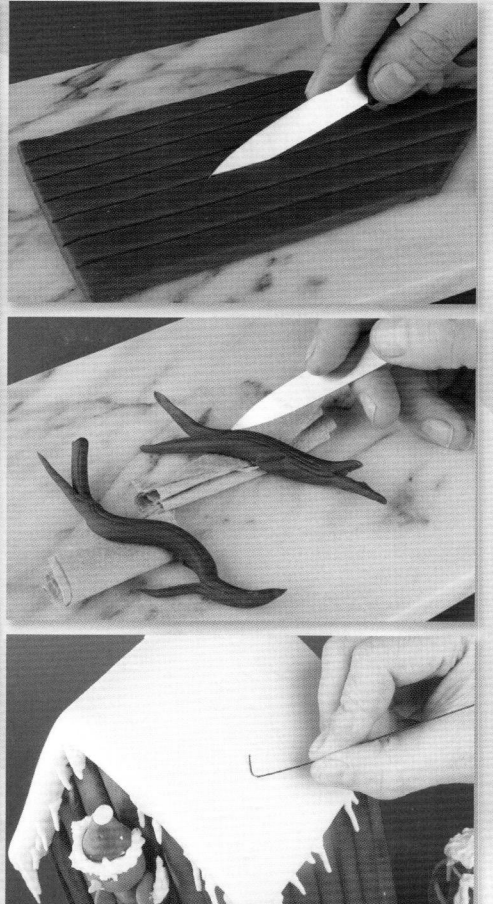

You will need:
10" Square cake sponge
10 Cupcakes in vanilla or chocolate sponge
35cm (14") Cake drum round
25cm (10") Cake drum round
10cm x 12cm (4"x 5") cake spacer round
1kg (2lb) Green sugarpaste
2kg (4lb) light brown sugarpaste
125g (4oz) yellow, grey, mauve, sugarpaste
1kg (2lb) Dark brown sugarpaste
Spray gun and colours
Craft knife

Firstly, cover the cake drums with green sugarpaste securing with edible glue.

Brush the sides of the cake spacer with edible glue and cover with dark brown sugarpaste.

For the branches, roll a sausage shape from sugarpaste cut slightly at one end you can now fix to the spacer. To give the bark effect start embossing the pattern using the back of a knife.

Preparation

Cut the square sponge cake in half and sandwich together, start shaping taking off a little at a time, you need to have a nice oval body when finished it should look like a large egg shape.

1 Mask the body with filling cream, cover with light brown sugarpaste and place onto the green cake board.
2 Start adding the legs and arms roll a sausage shape with sugarpaste, mark the paws with a craft knife, place onto the body securing with edible glue.
3 To make the head, mould sugarpaste into a pear shape, flatten with palms of hands and secure to the cake. Make two balls and flatten for the cheeks. Poke with the end of a paint brush for the eyes and then pipe with royal icing. For the lion's mane roll a strip of sugarpaste making it thicker one end and thinner the other, this helps it stay up and not fall, start cutting very narrow strips with a knife and secure the thicker end onto the head.

4 Start marking the fur effect by embossing with the back of a knife, covering all the cake including the head.
5 Start colouring the lion with a spray gun to give it more definition using a mixture of brown and white.
6 Making the cupcake animals, you will need two cupcakes for each animal, one of which is turned upside down and masked with filling cream, cover this with sugarpaste and place on top of the other cupcake. Roll a small ball of sugarpaste then press with your thumb to form a dip and place on top of the iced cupcake, this is very important it stops the head from falling off; giving extra support you do this on all the cupcakes.
7 Making the cupcake animals, most of the heads for the animals are made in the same way. To make the hippopotamus roll a ball mould into a pear shape and press the middle with your finger, add the ears and a small tail, pipe the eyes with royal icing.

King of the Jungle *continued*

For the lion cupcake: for the paws, roll a small ball press this with your finger and thumb secure onto cake, pipe the eyes with royal icing.

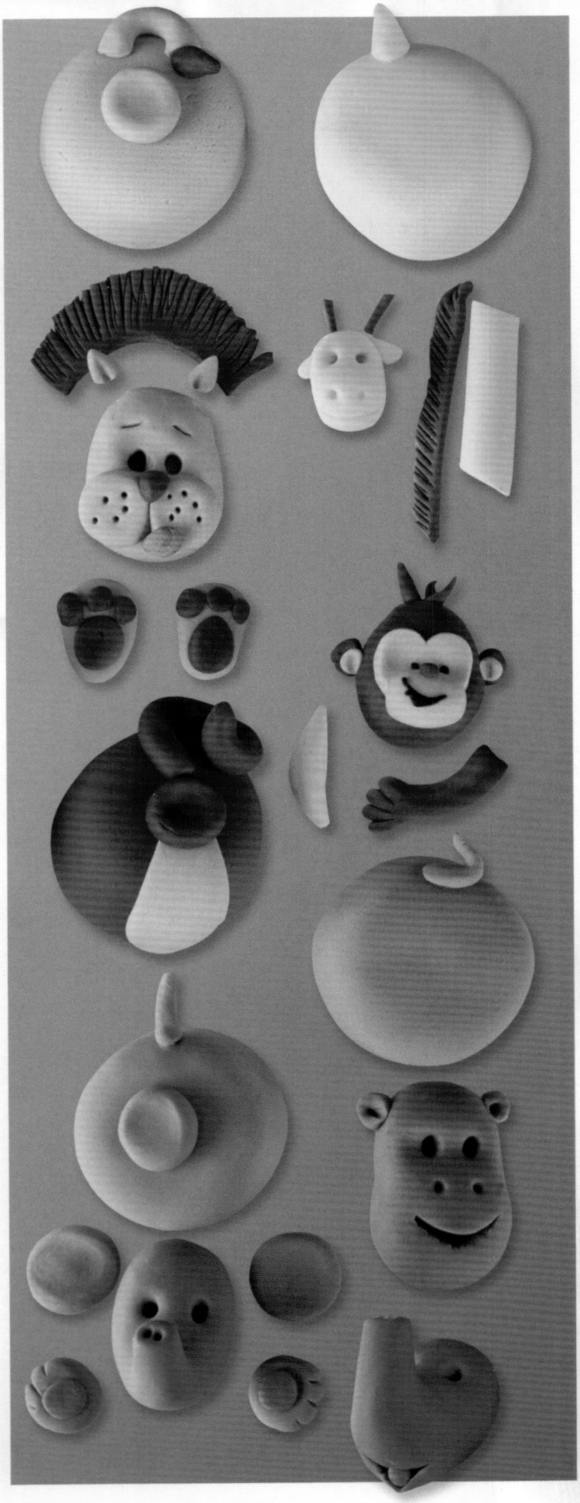

When making the giraffe, roll a sausage and shape the head, attach to the cupcake using a piece of hard spaghetti as a support. Paint the markings with watered down brown food colouring.

For the elephant roll a ball of sugarpaste, mould this into a pear shape, keep rolling to form the trunk, roll a ball for the ears and start flattening with your finger and thumb.

Add a little white to brown sugarpaste for the features on the monkey, make the arms a little longer, put a banana in his hand this all adds to the theme.

Finishing touches: roll out green sugarpaste and cut out leaves with a leaf shape cutter, start securing around the lion.

Finally, set your cake up, place cupcake animals onto the stand.

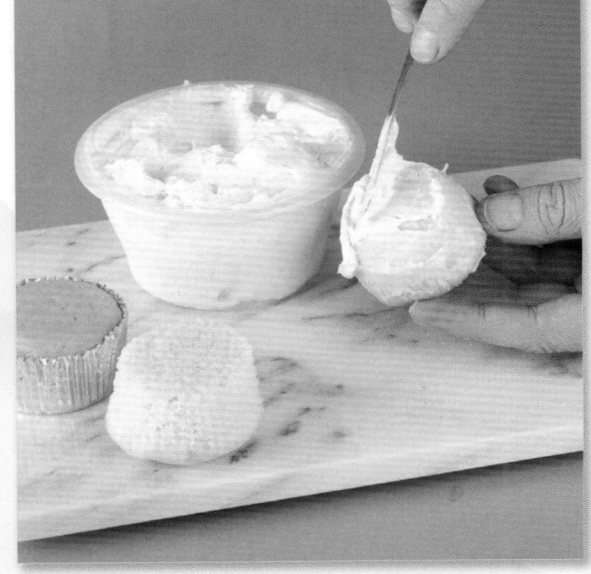

You will need,
25cm (10") round fruit cake
20cm (8") round fruit cake
15cm (6") round fruit cake
10cm (4") round fruit cake
4.4kg (10lb) marzipan
5kg (10lb10oz) white sugarpaste
Apricot jam for masking
Plastic cake dowel rods
Food colour for painting
Cake smoother
Craft knife
Paint brush

Firstly, cover the cake drum with sugarpaste, smooth and trim the edges.

Preparation

Place all the cakes onto double thick cake boards the same sizes as the cakes. Marzipan and ice the four fruit cakes, you can use sponge cakes but it is advisable to freeze for an hour or so to keep it nice and firm.
I tend to leave for twenty four hours before stacking them; using plastic dowel rods once inserted into the cake and cut to size, secure each cake on to the other with royal icing.
I will also pipe around the base of each cake with royal icing to seal.

To make the fabric drape

Roll a sheet of white sugarpaste; remember to make enough to go down two of the cakes, leaving a little more for trimming if necessary. Make two and place a plastic sheet over one while working on the other.

Place three dowel rods onto your work surface, place your rolled sugarpaste on top of them. This will give the ruffle effect, pinch each end of the drape and carefully attach to the cake securing with edible glue.

Continue to do the same with the second piece, trim the end and leave to dry before finishing.

Painting on the drape: mix a little clear alcohol with food colour, and carefully paint the details onto the drape, I have chosen roses but you can take designs from a piece of material or bridesmaid dress. Pipe royal icing with a No 2 tube to give a little more definition this also gives an embossed feel.

Finishing touches: roll a long thin sausage shape from white sugarpaste, place onto the base of each cake securing with edible glue, hiding the join behind the drape.

With a No 2 tube pipe royal icing pearl dots, just above the strip at the base of the cake.

Finally, place on to the cake, flowers of your choice; Make them quite large for the top, keeping it slightly smaller for the middle. Adding greenery like ivy breaks up the colours, keep it quite simple and not to overpowering.

Attach ribbon to match the signature theme of the cake.

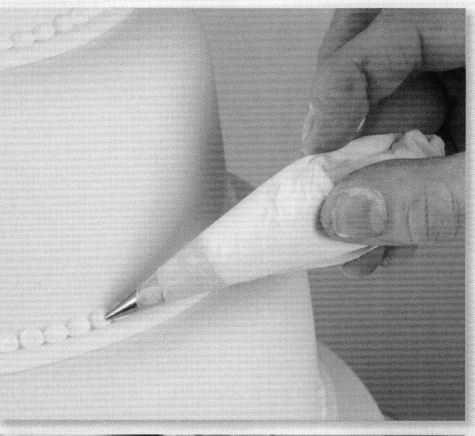

You will need:
20cm (8") Round sponge cake
30cm (12") Cake drum Round
1kg (2lb) lemon coloured sugarpaste
250g (8oz) Green coloured sugarpaste
250g (8oz) Pale green coloured sugarpaste
125g (4oz) Pink coloured sugarpaste
250g (8oz) white sugarpaste
Small amount of Orange, Deep pink, blue sugarpaste,
Royal icing

Firstly, roll out and cover the cake drum with pale green
sugarpaste.

Preparation

Jam and cream the cake and mask with filling cream, roll
out some pale lemon sugarpaste and cover the cake
smoothing with a cake smoother. Place the cake onto the
cake board, leave for two hours before starting to finish off.

1 Roll green sugarpaste and cut out a long strip, using a
   craft knife start cutting the grass shapes.
2 Attach the grass to the base of the cake, with a paint
   brush start brushing the grass to give it movement.
3 Roll green sugarpaste and cut out a 4inch round disk,
   secure this onto the middle of cake.

To make the rabbit

Roll a ball of sugarpaste and mould into a pear shape,
securing with edible glue attach this to the cake. Using
hard spaghetti as a support place this through the body,
leave for two hours.

For the arms and legs, roll sugarpaste into a sausage
shape, tweak the end to form the hands and cut the finger
with a craft knife. For the feet mould sugarpaste into a pear
shape roll slightly to make it longer, press this with your
finger and thumb to flatten.

Making the head: roll sugarpaste into a ball attach this on to
the body, make a smaller ball and place onto the middle of
the face, With a craft knife mark the details onto the face.

Secure the bunny's ears on to the head, pipe the eyes add
blusher on to the cheeks.

To make the Easter egg

Roll pastillage and place into a small Easter egg mould
leave to set for 24 hours, using royal icing attach the two
halves together. Start decorating the egg, I have used strips
of sugarpaste and piped small pearls with royal icing using
a No 2 tube.

Finishing touches: pipe on the grass around the rabbit,
I have not used a piping tube for this, just cut a small hole
into a piping bag and use the pressure piping method, do
the same to finish the base of the cake.

Just by piping little dots with royal icing in various colours,
you are creating little flowers.

Finally, add a small handmade butterfly securing with
royal icing.

High Fashion

You will need,

25cm (10") Sponge cake
15cm (6") Sponge cake
10cm (4") square Sponge cake
40cm (15") Cake drum round
15cm (6") Double thick cake card
25cm (10") Double thick cake card
1.8kg (4lb) Marzipan
2kg (4lb4oz) Royal icing
1kg (2lb) Black sugarpaste
Gold dusting powder
Rejuvenating spirit
Edible glaze spray

Firstly, cover the 15" cake drum with black sugarpaste, leave aside to be used later.

Preparation

Mask with boiled apricot jam and marzipan the two cakes, doing the sides first and then the top so the edges are nice and square.

1 Start royal icing the two cakes, using a paddling motion on the top of the cake this helps to take the air bubbles away. Coat the first coat of royal icing quite thin, once coated leave for 24 hours before attempting the side coats.
2 Two to three coats of icing is needed, waiting at least 24 hours between coats, a good surface is required and nice sharp edges for this cake if you achieve this, it will not need elaborate decoration it is often the simple designs that I think look the best.
3 Place the finished royal iced cake on to the black iced cake board. Dowel and place the smaller cake on top securing with royal icing.
5 Using black royal icing in a piping bag fitted with a No 2 tube, start piping lace work I haven't set a design for this cake, I just let my imagination run wild.

How to make the handbag

Cut the 4" 10cm sponge cake in half and sandwich together. Start trimming from the top and work your way down not taking too much off at a time keep trimming till you achieve the bag shape mask with filling cream and chill in a refrigerator till firm.

Cover with black sugarpaste trim the edges, Start adding the trimmings onto the bag, just by adding small strips of sugarpaste and the padlock will make it look authentic.

To make the handle, I have used black pastillage and left this to dry for 24 hours; I have then attached this to the bag using a small amount of black royal icing as glue. You will need some support while waiting for it to set; polystyrene blocks are a good option.

Spray the bag with edible glaze to give it the leather look, and place this onto the top of the cake.

Finishing touches, roll sugarpaste very thin and ruffle as you place this around the bag, add a drape coming down to the next tier. Make a paint by mixing gold dusting powder with rejuvenating spirit and paint the fabric.

Finally, pipe small pearls in black around edge of the cake board, finish by securing ribbon to edge of the board.

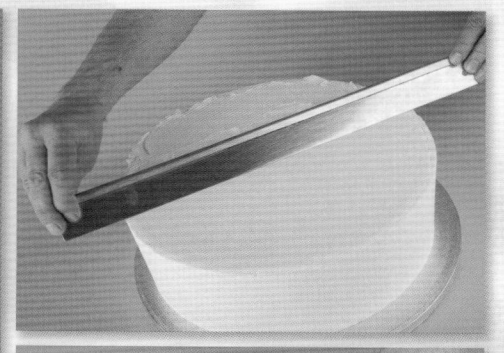

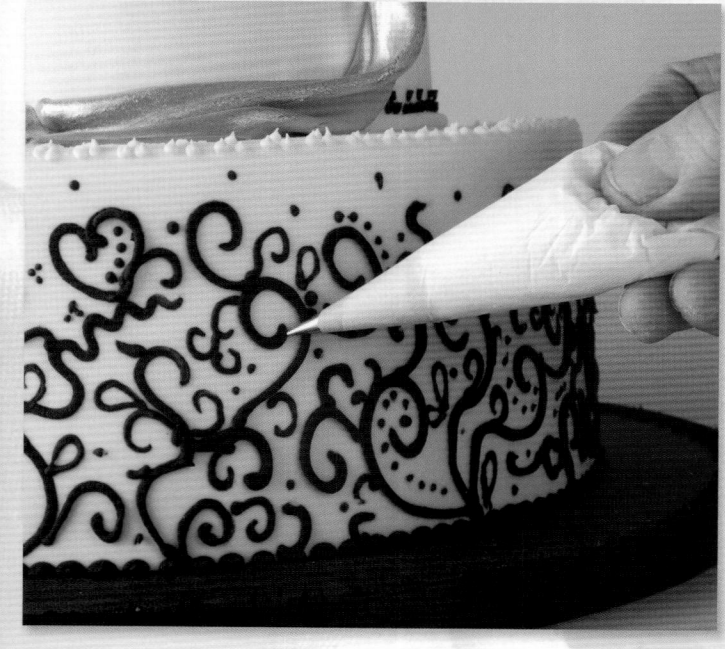

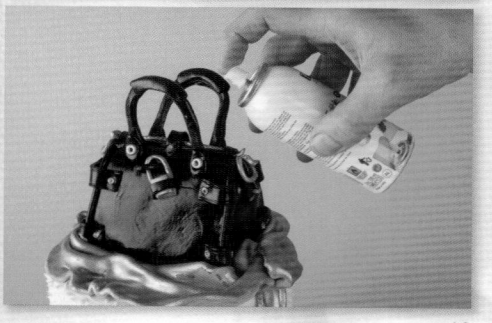

Fun in the Snow

You will need,
35cm (14") Cake drum round
Sponge cake baked in a small ball baking tin
Rice krispy treats
2kg (4lb4oz) White sugarpaste
250g (8oz) Dark blue sugarpaste
125g (4oz) red sugarpaste
75g (2oz) Orange sugarpaste
125g (4oz) green sugarpaste
125g (4oz) Black sugarpaste
250g (8oz) Royal icing

Firstly, cover the cake board with sugarpaste leave aside to be used later.

Preparation

Roll out some white sugarpaste and cover the ball shaped cake, and place this onto the iced cake board.

1 Build up the back of the cake board with sugarpaste, this is to help balance the head.
2 Using rice krispy treats mould into a round ball for the head, cover this in sugarpaste the same way as the body.
3 Put the head in place, you may need a little more sugarpaste to help position the head.
4 Making arms and legs: roll out a sausage shape with white sugarpaste, Fix onto the body using a plastic dowel rod cut to size for support.
5 To make the feet mould sugarpaste into a pear shape and flatten with the palms of your hands, secure onto the legs with edible glue.
6 Cut a strip of rolled green sugarpaste and secure around the snowman's neck, cut strips of red sugarpaste, place onto the scarf.
7 Make the hat by rolling some dark blue sugarpaste and cutting a round circle shape, position into place.
   For the rim of the hat cut a strip of sugarpaste a little thicker and secure into place.

How to make the penguin

Mould black sugarpaste into a pear shape for the body, roll a ball for the head and position in place. Mould two pear shapes and flatten for the wings.

With rolled out white sugarpaste and using a small heart cutter, cut out a heart shape and place onto the face, mould a small amount to place onto the body. Finish by adding the feet and a small beak, pipe the eyes with royal icing.

Finishing touches: add some handmade holly to his hat, give him a carrot nose, and brush the cheeks using edible dusting powder. Pipe the eyes and mouth using royal icing.

Finally, using royal icing and a palate knife, start to stipple just under where the snowman's head is positioned, Finish off by covering the whole board with edible glitter flakes.

Box of Delights

You will need,
35cm (14") Square cake drum
25cm (10") Square sponge cake
15cm (6") Round sponge cake
15cm (6") Double thick cake card round
15cm x 2.5cm (6"x 1") polystyrene cake spacer
1.5kg (3lb) Pink coloured sugarpaste
500g (1lb2oz) Teal coloured sugarpaste
Small amounts of, yellow and purple sugarpaste
250g (8oz) readymade pastillage
Pearl white shimmer dusting powder
Rejuvenating spirit
Small amount of royal icing

Firstly, cover the cake drum with white sugarpaste, leave this aside to be used later.

Preparation

Jam and cream the two cakes and mask them with filling cream. Put them into the freezer for one hour before attempting to cover them.

1 Roll out pink sugarpaste into a large sheet, place the top of the cake on top of this and trim around, Do the same with the sides one at a time, when you have finished you should be left with a nice square box shape. Place this on to the iced square cake drum.
2 To make the lid for the square cake, make an oblong template half an inch smaller than the box but the same length as one side. Roll out a sheet of pink sugarpaste place this on top of the cake securing with edible glue. Using the template as a guide, start trimming the access.
3 For the ribbon roll out some pastillage quite thin and cut two strips, secure onto the square box using edible glue.
4 Roll out a sheet of teal coloured sugarpaste, place the top of the round cake on top of this and trim. For the sides you need to cut out a strip this will be placed around the side, and carefully trim the edges, place this onto the double thick board.
5 Position the round cake onto the square cake securing with royal icing.
6 Place strips of yellow, teal, purple and pink sugarpaste on to the sides of the round cake, cutting different sizes, securing using edible glue.
7 Roll a sheet pastillage and ruffle this as you place this on to the top of the round cake. Leave to set for two hours.
8 Cover the cake spacer with teal coloured sugarpaste and position in place.

How to make the bows

Roll a sheet of pastillage quite thinly, and cut-out strips all the same size, cut this in half, Fold each piece of the bow till it meets, place tissue paper into the bow as a support and leave to set overnight. To give the ribbon a flowing effect, I placed tissue paper underneath the pastillage strips and leave to set over night.

Once set, position your bows in place securing with royal icing.

Finishing touches, with a No 2 tube pipe the pattern on top of the square box this will give it an embossed look.

Make a lustre paint by mixing edible pearl white dusting powder with rejuvenating spirit carefully paint this onto the ribbons and bows.

Finally, finish your cake by piping clean lines around the top of the base cake board using a No 2 piping nozzle.

Fix ribbon onto the side of the cake drum.

Rose Cottage

You will need,
2 x 25cm (10") Sponge cakes
35cm (14") Cake drum square
1kg (2lb) White sugarpaste
1kg (2lb) Light brown sugarpaste
250g (8oz) Grey sugarpaste
500g (1lb2oz) green sugarpaste
Small amounts of various coloured sugarpaste
Small amount of pastillage
250g (8oz) Royal icing
Sieve
Cobble stone mould (FMM)
Spray gun and colours

Firstly, cover the cake drum with green sugarpaste, leave aside for later.

Preparation

Cut the cakes in half and sandwich two of them together, measure and cut so its 20cm (8") long, repeat the same method for the other two halves. Start trimming the roof and give it more of a rounded edge, once completed mask with filling cream place in freezer for 1 hour to firm.
With the spare sponge cut out the roof windows and the entrance porch of the cottage.

1 Roll out white sugarpaste into a large sheet, place the top of the cake on top of this and trim around, do the same with each side one at a time. When you have finished you will be left with an oblong box shape.
2 Place the roof windows on to the cake and cover the roof with light brown sugarpaste, cutting around the windows, place this on to the oblong cake, along with the entrance porch.
3 Using the fmm strip cutter cut a long strip with light brown sugarpaste, cut either side so it is a mirror image and place this on top of the roof.
4 With the back of a knife start marking the thatch affect onto the roof.
5 Mould a small square for the chimney with sugarpaste and mark a brick design by free hand, cut a V shape at the bottom and place onto the roof.
6 Start to spray the roof with yellow first and then over spray with brown, using a spray gun.

7 Make a small square template, cut around to make holes for the windows. Roll some black sugarpaste, using the same square template cut around, place the sugarpaste squares into the holes making the windows. Make the doorway in the same way, using green sugarpaste and making an oblong template.
8 Pipe the window frames using a No 2 piping tube with grey royal icing, add the window ledges with small strips of black sugarpaste.

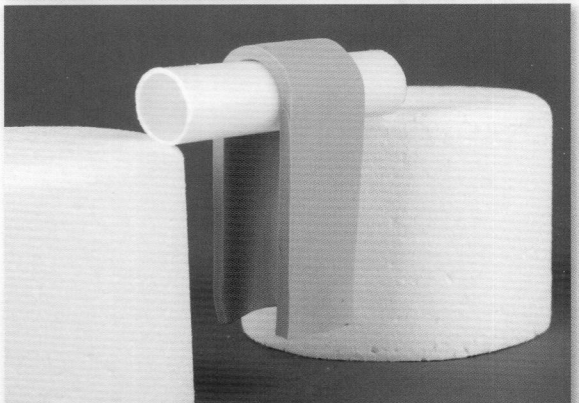

Creating the landscaped garden

To make the cobble stoned wall cut a thick strip of grey sugarpaste press the fmm cobble stone mould into this, secure onto the cake with edible glue, remembering to leave a space for the rose arch.

How to make all the trees and bushes

Using a sieve, press various coloured sugarpaste through and place around the garden. Mould some cones and cut with a pair of scissors working from the bottom working your way up, to form the trees.

I have used many different colours with royal icing and piped small flowers onto the bushes.

How to make the rose arch

With a strip of brown coloured pastillage, shape this into the arch and leave to dry for 24 hours. When completely dry place on to the cake, make a leaf bag and start piping small leaves around the arch its best if you use two colours of green royal icing this makes it look more realistic. Finish by piping small roses around the arch.

Finishing touches, make a small bird bath from pastillage; I have made the water effect by using piping jelly. Make a small cat to sit on to the wall, all adds to the theme.

Finally, secure ribbon onto the cake drum.

It's a Dog's Life

You will need,
15cm (6") Square sponge cake
25cm (10") Cake drum square
Rice krispy treats
1.8kg (4lb) Light brown sugarpaste
250g (8oz) Dark blue sugarpaste
250g (8oz) White sugarpaste
Small amounts of purple, Green, Grey sugarpaste
Black sugarpaste
Craft knife

Firstly, Cover the cake drum with dark blue sugarpaste, trim and leave aside till later.

Preparation

Jam and cream the square cake, mask the sides and top with filling cream and put in the freezer for one hour to set.

1   Roll out a sheet of light brown sugarpaste, place the top of the cake on top and trim around. Do the same with each side so you are left with a square box shape.
2   Using the back of a long knife, start marking the sides of the box, giving it a wood panelling effect.
3   Place the cake onto the cake board, start spraying with brown food colour using a spay gun, shade in a little black for the darker areas.
4   Start making the dog, firstly mould a piece of sugarpaste for the part of the body showing, attach this to the box securing with edible glue.
5   I have moulded rice Krispy treats to make the dog's head, it's lighter than using solid sugarpaste so this helps it stay in place, especially when using sponge cakes.
6   I find it's better to study the dog, have a picture at hand, look at the features and adding the muscles were necessary, you're more likely to get a better likeness.
7   Brush the dogs face with edible glue and cover using light brown sugarpaste, carefully smooth with your hands.
8   Start creating the fur using the back of a knife, you will need to add small pieces of sugarpaste above the eyes for the eyebrows, and this will make it look fluffier.
10 Roll out light brown sugarpaste and cut out the ears, secure with edible glue.

11 Add the paws on to the box, start shading the detail with a spray gun using yellow and brown food colouring, spray around the mouth with black and shade where necessary. You will need to leave to dry for about 2 hours.
12 Roll out a sheet of white sugarpaste quite thinly, ruffle and place this around the dog.

Final touches: .Add the nose and eyes onto the dog securing with edible glue. Make the dog's collar and add a bow on to the head.

Finally, Make a ball using sugarpaste and place onto the board, create the dogs bone and the last final touch make a tongue and secure with edible glue.

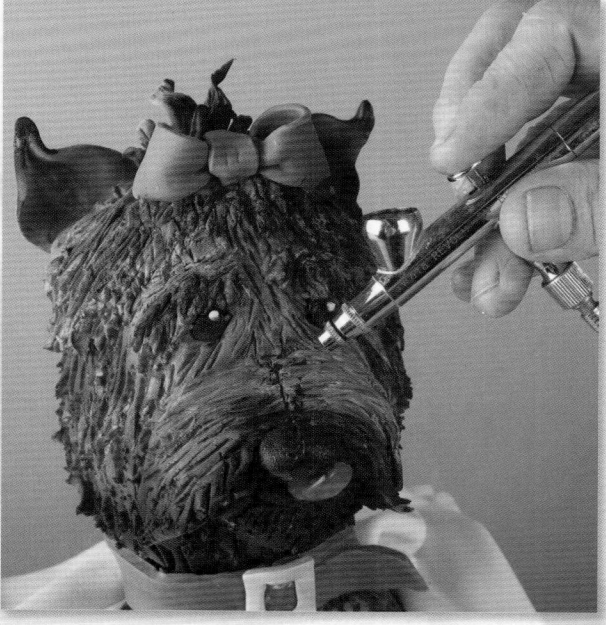

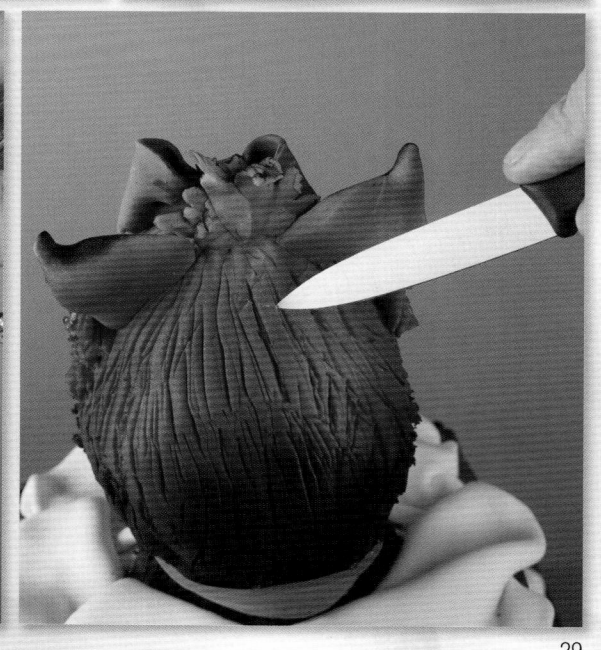

You will need,

30cm (12") Cake drum square
20cm (8") Sponge cake square
2kg (4.4lb) Black sugarpaste
1kg (2.2lb) White sugarpaste
250g (8oz) Pastillage
Small amounts of Blue, Pink, & Peach sugarpaste
Edible silver paint
 Royal icing in various colours
No5 Piping nozzle
Craft knife
Small square cutter 4cm (1.5")
Edible glaze spray

Firstly, roll out some black sugarpaste into a large sheet, start cutting out square shapes with a square cutter. Place these on to the cake board securing with edible glue.

To give the tiled floor a speckled effect, make up a paint solution using rejuvenating spirit with white edible powder, you then dip this into the paint and flick this onto the tiles, leave to dry.

Spray the tiles with edible glaze and leave to dry for 20 minutes, give this another coat and leave aside till later.

Preparation

Jam and cream the cake and cut it into three, cut one of the pieces in half. Mask the three pieces with filling cream, place in refrigerator for 1 hour to set.

1 To make the kitchen units: roll out white sugarpaste, place the cake onto this and cut around, you want it to have square edges, you do this on all four sides.
2 Turn the cake flat so it is facing you, and with rolled out sugarpaste start cutting the doors and draws of the units, you will find this a lot easier and it will look neater too. It would be advisable to have a little icing sugar on your work surface at this point.
3 Add the door knobs by rolling a small ball of sugarpaste, using the back of a paint brush, position in to place.
4 Place the cakes onto the cake board and position into place.
5 Using rolled black sugar paste cut out strips and place onto the tops of the units, smoothing the edges to give a slight rounded edge.

6 Cut out the shape for the oven and also the sink, by cutting into the icing on the cake so you are left with a hole. I have done this free hand but using a square cutter will do the job just as good. Roll out a thin piece of sugarpaste and fill in the holes, remember you want an indent so not to thick.
7 To make the cooker hob, cut a square of rolled sugarpaste to fit, securing with edible glue, Roll 4 various size small balls, press with your finger and thumb position into place, Pipe the gas jet covers with black royal icing using a No 2 tube.
8 Lightly spray the cake with edible glaze giving the units and top a shine.

Making the accessories

The cup cake stand: cut three various sized circles from pastillage, roll a sausage shape and cut to size for the spacers, leave to dry for 24 hours and attach together with royal icing.

The little bowls: roll a small ball of pastillage, press on to the top of a thick plastic dowel rod, roll slightly and trim with a craft knife. Once dry you can paint with edible silver paint, you can fill these with coloured royal icing, adding to the theme.

The food mixer: thickly roll out some pastillage, I have cut this out free hand but you can make yourself a small template if you wish. Leave this to dry flat for 24 hours; why not copy your own mixer.

The cupcake baking trays: cut oblong shapes from rolled pastillage, press to make the holes, with the back of a paint brush. Paint with silver edible paint, when dry pipe in your cupcakes with royal icing.

How to make the little cupcakes

Roll small balls of sugarpaste and flatten slightly, indent the sides of them with a craft knife to give a crimped effect. Paint with silver or gold edible paint, once dry pipe the icing swirls using a No 5 piping nozzle using royal icing.

How to make the figure

Although this figure looks like she is sitting on a block of icing for a good support. I tend to find looking at your own body is a great guide, why not try putting your arms by your side and just look how far down your legs they reach.

Roll a sausage from sugarpaste and cut into two for her jeans, secure with edible glue onto the block of icing, put a piece of hard spaghetti through this and leave for 3 hours.

Brush edible glue onto the hard spaghetti; mould some pink sugarpaste for the body, secure into place shaping slightly with your hands.

Roll a sausage when making the arms and cut into two and secure onto the body. Make the hands and place a little handmade piping bag in her hand.

Roll a small ball of sugarpaste for the head, press the centre with your finger to make an indent. Press with the end of a paint brush to indent the eyes, brush the cheeks with suitable edible dusting powder.

Secure onto the body, pipe the eyes into place using royal icing, pipe on her hair using royal icing, and finish with cutting her mouth using a craft knife.

Finally make her apron and attach to the body making a small bow at the back.

Finishing touches: fill the sink with dishes, using some extra accessories you have made, achieve a water effect using a little piping jelly. Make some extra cupcakes in different shapes, pipe onto these using royal icing and place nto position.

Finally, attach a suitable colour ribbon on the sides of the cake board.

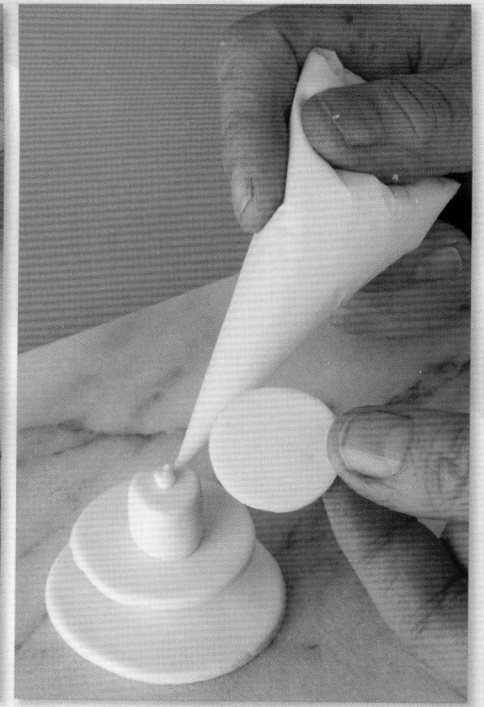

You will need:
20cm (8") Sponge cake round
30cm (12") Cake drum round
500g (1lb) White sugarpaste
250g (8oz) Orange sugarpaste
Various colours of petal paste
Various colours of sugarpaste
24g gold metallic wires
Small amount of white royal icing
Round cutter shape
No 2 piping nozzle

Preparation

Jam and cream the cake mask with filling cream and leave this in a refrigerator for 2 hours to firm.

1 Roll out a sheet of white sugarpaste place the top of the cake on top of this and trim, carefully smooth this with a cake smoother.
2 For the sides roll out a strip of black sugarpaste a little larger than the side of the cake. Carefully place this onto the side of the cake smoothing gently with a cake smoother at the same time. Trim the edges till you have a sharp finish to your cake.
3 Position the iced cake onto the cake board, I tend to leave over night at this point. It's much easier to work with.
4 Roll out strips of orange sugarpaste very thinly, you will find making fabric effect works best if your paste is rolled thinly. You will need to pleat the icing together to form the ruffles, carefully place this onto the cake drum securing with edible glue.
5 Start to cut out circles using various colours of rolled sugarpaste. Secure onto the cake as picture, leaving a slight space between each one.
6 Using white sugarpaste roll small sausage shapes, make one end a little thinner so it resembles an elongated pear shape. Carefully place on to the cake in-between each of the circles, securing each one into place using edible glue.
7 Roll little balls about the size of a small pea shape, secure onto the cake as seen in the picture.

Finishing touches: roll small ball shapes using various colours of pastillage. Dip the 24g gold metallic wires into edible glue, thread the wire through the ball till it's half way,, do this with all the ball shapes and leave to set for 24 hours.

Fill a large posy pick with pastillage, push into the centre of the cake till it is level. Carefully place the wired balls into the posy pick. Once all in place you can hide the posy pick by piping royal icing or a sugarpaste pattern.

Finally, finish by piping loops under the circle shapes, using royal icing fitted with a no2 piping nozzle. Secure ribbon onto the cake drum using a colour that suits the theme.

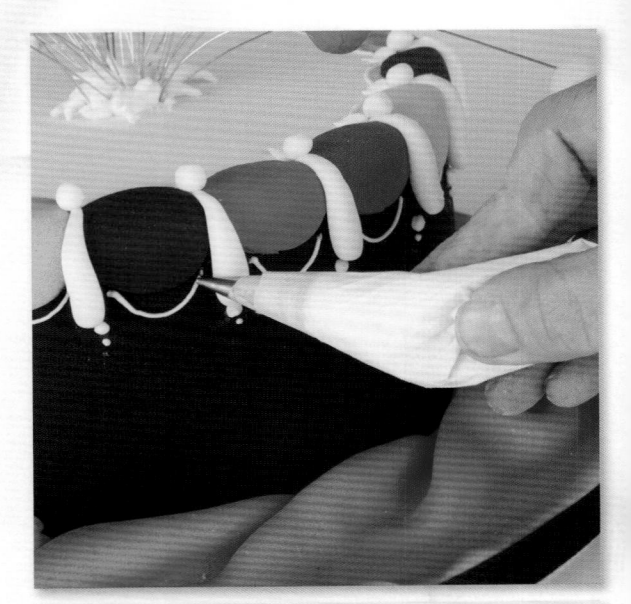

Swan Lake

You will need:
10cm (4") Round sponge cake
32 Sponge Cupcakes
3kg (6lb) Deep Red coloured sugarpaste
15cm (6") gold round cake drum
16 White suitable cake wraps
250g (8oz) pastillage
Rejuvenating spirit
Small amount of royal icing
Edible bright gold dusting powder
A suitable 4 tier cupcake stand
Paint brush

How to make the domed cupcakes

1 You will need two cup cakes to make each one of these.
   Firstly take the outer wrapping from the cupcake and
   turn upside down, start trimming not taking too much till
   you have formed a dome shape.
2 Cream the domed cupcake with filling cream, you will
   need to mask sixteen of these. It's best to place these in
   a refrigerator for 2 hours before attempting to cover them.
3 Roll out the red sugarpaste and start to cut rounds with
   a circle cutter, make sure it is slightly larger than the size
   of the domed cupcake.
4 Place on to the domed cupcake carefully smoothing with
   a cake smoother. You will find doing it this way not only
   saves you time but also gives you a neater finish.
5 Cream the top of the foiled cupcake, place the dome on
   top of this and leave for 2 hours before finishing.
6 Colour royal icing using old gold food colour and place
   this into a piping bag fitted with a no2 tube.
7 Start to pipe whirls with the piping bag, this is a simple
   design but very effective, a good tip is to practice on a
   work board first this will also help you get into a rhythm.
8 When the piped whirls are fully dry you can start to paint
   them, firstly add rejuvenating spirit to the gold dusting
   powder till you have formed a paint solution. Using a fine
   paint brush carefully paint the whirls making sure not to
   touch the cake in the process.
9 Fix the cake wraps around, ready to be placed onto the
   cake stand.

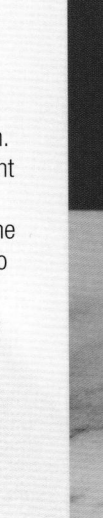

How to make the top cake

Cover the small cake with red sugarpaste, leave this over night, I find working on cakes that have been left for twenty four hours easier to work with and a lot better than trying to work on a cake that has soft sugarpaste on it.

To make the swans, roll out some pastillage and using the template provided start to cut around using a craft knife, you need to make two of these the other being a mirror image. You will also have to cut 2 wings using a leaf cutter, a good tip is to make spares in case or breakages, Leave to dry for 24 hours.

Start to pipe using a No 2 piping tube with white royal icing start piping a design of your choice onto the swans, leave to dry before attempting to handle it.

Place the swans onto the top cake securing with white royal icing, you will need some support I used small polystyrene blocks to do this, only remove when fully set.

Finishing touches: Cut out small hearts and place onto the base of the cake securing with edible glue, using royal icing and a No 2 tube start to pipe small hearts once these are dry, paint gold.

Finally, place the cupcakes onto the stand and carefully place the small cake onto the top.

Use this Swan template
Dimensions: Height 11cm Width 8cm

You will need:

2 x 20cm (8") Round fruit cakes
2 x 15cm (6") Round fruit cakes
35cm (14") Round cake drum
1.8kg (4lb) Marzipan
1.8kg (4lb) Turquoise blue sugarpaste (you will have to colour this yourself)
450g (1lb) White sugarpaste
425g (8oz) Pastillage
Large butterfly cutter
Small butterfly plunger cutter
Royal icing for piping
No 1.5 piping tube
No 2 piping tube

Firstly, Roll out some pastillage, using the large butterfly cutter and emboss the pattern on top. With a piece of card fold in half and place the butterfly onto this and leave to set for 24 hours.

It is advisable to roll the pastillage quite thin this way it will stay on the cake and not be too heavy.

Preparation

Sandwich the two cakes together securing with boiled apricot jam.

Marzipan and cover the two cakes, place the larger of the two onto the cake board which has been covered with white sugarpaste. Dowel the cake and place the smaller one on top.

1 Using a plastic dowel press into the white sugarpaste on the base of the cake board to give it the ruffled effect.
2 Roll out the sugarpaste and cut out butterfly's using a small butterfly plunger cutter.
3 Secure the cut out butterflies' onto the top edge of each of the two cakes, using edible glue.
4 Use a No 2 piping tube with turquoise coloured royal icing, pipe around the outside of each of the butterflies, continue to pipe the centre design using the embossed pattern as a guide.
5 with white royal icing and using a no2 piping tube, Start piping small pearls around the bottom edge of the base cake, start piping more here and there graduating them upwards. Do the same on the second tier using turquoise coloured royal icing.

6 Pipe graduating pearls onto the centre of each butterfly.
7 Add a little icing sugar to some royal icing, to make it a little stiffer, place into a piping bag and use as a glue to stick the larger butterflies on to the cake, leave to set for two hours before attempting to pipe on to it.
8 Using a No 1.5 piping tube, start to pipe the lace effect, I have used the embossed pattern on the butterfly as a guide, piping filigree around the inside edge, start to pipe small pearls and flowers. Small loops are piped around the edge to give it a more lacey look.

Finishing touches: secure the ribbon onto the side of the cake drum.

Finally, place the finished cake on to a suitable cake stand, adding a nice touch to your creation.